GOING HOME

MEDITATIONS ON FINISHING THE RACE

Going Home

Meditations on Finishing the Race

by J. D. Ashcroft

AMBASSADOR INTERNATIONAL
GREENVILLE, SOUTH CAROLINA & BELFAST, NORTHERN IRELAND

www.ambassador-international.com

GOING HOME

Meditations on Finishing the Race

PRINTED IN THE UNITED STATES OF AMERICA

ISBN 978-1-935507-03-1

COVER DESIGN & PAGE LAYOUT BY DAVID SIGLIN OF A&E MEDIA

AMBASSADOR INTERNATIONAL
EMERALD HOUSE
427 WADE HAMPTON BLVD.
GREENVILLE, SC 29609, USA
WWW.AMBASSADOR-INTERNATIONAL.COM

AMBASSADOR PUBLICATIONS
PROVIDENCE HOUSE
ARDENLEE STREET
BELFAST, BT6 8QJ, NORTHERN IRELAND, UK
WWW.AMBASSADOR-PRODUCTIONS.COM

THE COLOPHON IS A TRADEMARK OF AMBASSADOR

DEDICATION

This book is dedicated to Jesus Christ my Lord, who is our Savior from death. It is also given in memory of all those I love who have 'gone home' before me; my grandparents, parents, and Christian friends. For Jesus, and for them, I give thanks and praise to Almighty God, the giver of every perfect gift!

TABLE OF CONTENTS

PREFACE

Life and death are experienced by all of us, but we normally focus on one of them, and try to exclude the other from our minds as long as possible. Our modern culture focuses upon the therapeutic preservation of life so much that very little time is spent considering the fact that we all experience death, and should prepare for it as faithfully as we should prepare for, say, the birth of a child.

Death is considered a morbid topic, but it is only such for those who have no hope beyond physical death. This devotional is written for Christians, who consider death a gateway through which we enter eternal life. If these meditations are read in conjunction with humane programs like Hospice, the Christian can receive comfort and encouragement at this difficult period in their lives, and hopefully be better prepared for the reality that they will experience.

It is my prayer in writing these meditations that God would be glorified, and you, my reader, might be blessed and comforted. God bless you and prepare you for meeting Him in glory!

I

THE NECESSITY OF FAITH

"I am the resurrection and the life. Whoever believes in me, though he die,
yet shall he live, and everyone who lives and believes in me shall never die."
John 11:25-26
Do you believe this?

You have just heard the hardest news of your life: your condition is terminal, without remedy. After all the surgeries and treatments for illnesses and conditions the time has come to accept the reality that you are facing death. You are going to die. This truth is very difficult to bear.

How can we cope with this news? As Christians, we are called to trust in Jesus as our Lord and Savior from the fear of death. We must go back to the beginning of our faith, and cling to the promises that our Lord has given to us. Let us look at what Jesus says in these verses.

He says "I am the resurrection and the life." Jesus is the embodiment of the resurrection, in that he restores us from death by his resurrection from the dead. We must die as a result of our unity with Adam; but we will rise from death to life because of our unity with Christ. (Rom. 5:17)

How can Christ be the source of our resurrection? He says "Whoever believes in me, though he die, yet shall he live." We must believe in Jesus as our Savior, who died in our place, if we are to experience victory over death. Faith is the one necessary requirement for this miracle to take place. The faith to believe that what Jesus did on the cross was for us, and that his resurrection is proof of his victory over death, is itself a gift of God's grace (Eph. 2:8).

Jesus is also "the life". He says that "everyone who lives and believes in me shall never die." The life that Jesus has given us in his resurrection is a well-spring which will last forever; it is eternal life. We live forever because Christ lives in us, and keeps us in his grasp for all time. Jesus tells us that "My sheep hear my voice, and I know them, and they follow me. I give them eternal life, and they will never perish, and no one will snatch them out of my hand"(Jn. 10:27-8).

Here is our greatest comfort when facing the reality of death: Jesus has overcome death by his death and resurrection for us. He has promised that we will never die if we believe in him.

Jesus said to Martha: "Do you believe this?" This is the question which we must answer in order to prepare for death. Do we believe in Jesus, the one who conquered death for us by dying in our place? If we believe this, then we are ready to face the hard reality of earthly death, the death of our body. This is a difficult experience, but it is surmountable because Jesus has promised us both the resurrection of our bodies and the eternal life of our souls.

Let us therefore be thankful that we can face our future death because Jesus has had victory over it on our behalf.

Dear Lord, we pray that you would grant us faith in your promise to us, that if we believe in you we will live in spite of experiencing the death of our earthly bodies. Help us trust in your victory on our behalf, In Jesus Name, amen.

2

THE COMFORT JESUS GIVES

"Let not your heart be troubled: Believe in God; believe also in me. In my Father's house are many rooms. If it were not so, would I have told you that I go to prepare a place for you? And if I go and prepare a place for you, I will come again and will take you to myself, that where I am you may be also."
John 14:1-3

It is a shock for us to be informed of terminal illness. Thankfully, our Lord has given wonderful comfort to enable us to face the trial before us. Here in this text our Lord has just announced to his disciples that He would be leaving them soon. Instead of focusing upon the cross and suffering to come, Jesus comforted his disciples. These three verses contain some of the most enduring comfort in all of sacred literature. In them Jesus exhorts his disciples to believe in God, to believe in Him, and believe that He will come again to be with them forever.

Jesus comforted his disciples by an exhortation to faith in God. "Let not your hearts be troubled. Believe in God." The disciples' hearts were indeed "troubled", or agitated by the news he had just given them. Not only was Jesus to leave them, Peter, one of their leaders, would deny the Lord three times (John 13:31-38). In this context Jesus gives them a word of comfort, and a message which would see them through their trial. Jesus exhorted them to "believe", which means "to place our trust in someone." Who did Jesus exhort them to trust? God. No greater counsel can be given to disquieted souls than to place our trust in the Lord. God is "our God forever and ever. He will guide us forever." (Ps. 48:14). God will never leave us or forsake us (Heb. 13:5). He is worthy of all our trust at all times.

Jesus also comforted his disciples by exhorting them to believe in him. "Believe also in me." Jesus wanted his disciples to trust him, and place faith in his words to them. In this case he tells them of a work he will perform while absent from them. He says: "In my Father's house are many rooms. If it were not so, would I have told you that I go to prepare a place for you?" Here our Lord makes clear that His life will not be limited by physical death. He also tells them that there is a place in the heavens, a mansion composed of many rooms, owned by God. Moreover, Jesus tells His followers that he is going to that mansion to "prepare a place" for *them*.

Death is a fearful event. It is also a fearful thing to stand before a holy, omniscient, and just God. Jesus went to the cross in order to eliminate our fear of both of these events. Moreover, he has promised us "a place", a room in the palace of Almighty God. Jesus, the Son of the Father, went to heaven to prepare for our arrival there! There is no greater comfort for disciples of Christ than to know that He has made a way for us to be welcome at the throne of God.

Jesus also comforted his disciples by promising to return for them. He says "I will come again and will take you to myself, that where I am you may be also." Here is the first time in the Scripture that Jesus promises that he will return to earth. In the second coming of our Lord, we will be re-united with our Lord, and have fellowship with Him. The most painful part of grief is separation. Jesus defuses that agony with the promise that we shall see Him again. Moreover, implicit in this promise is that God's mansion will be filled with others, who, like His disciples, put their trust in God, and in the work of His Son, Jesus Christ our Lord. If we have a place in the mansion of God, we shall be re-united with all believers who have gone before us; whether Apostles, parents, children or friends.

This great word of comfort brings to the forefront the single most important need we have: We need to believe in God our Father, and the work of Jesus Christ, His only Son and our Lord. If we would only place our faith in the Lord, we will find that we are promised a place in God's heavenly house, with all our believing loved ones.

Dear Lord, grant us the grace of belief, that we might not fear our death, but look forward to our life in heaven with you and all our Christian loved ones. In Jesus Name, amen.

3
REMEMBER YOUR FORGIVENESS

"And you, who were dead in your trespasses and the uncircumcision of your flesh, God made alive together with him, having forgiven us all our trespasses, by canceling the record of debt that stood against us with its legal demands. This he set aside, nailing it to the cross."
Col. 2:13-14

During our times of trial it is possible for us to think about our failures and wonder whether God will forgive our worst sins. We feel guilty for sins long ago confessed and forgiven. These thoughts can plague us and cause great depression during our final illness. These thoughts must be rejected on the basis of God's Word: we must remember that God has forgiven us.

Paul says here that we were once "dead" in our trespasses, but that we are now "alive together with Christ." Our belief is that Jesus has delivered us from spiritual death and liberated us from the consequences of sin. We have been raised us to life through faith in the power of God, who raised Jesus from the dead. (Col. 2:12) We have this blessing because of what Jesus has done for us.

Moreover, because of the cross, we are forgiven for our sins. Paul says "having forgiven us all our trespasses, by canceling the record of debt which stood against us with its legal demands, *this he set aside, nailing it to the cross."*

This blessing of God to us is enormous. Yes, we are sinners and have sinned against God. Yet He has removed the charges against us by canceling the list of sins we have committed. These he has "set aside," or more literally, "blotted out." Praise God for this Word of comfort! There is now no more record of our sins before the throne of God! He has erased the charge-list of our sins; they have been deleted from our record, entirely removed! Let us therefore no longer submit to self-condemnation, when God Himself has chosen to remember our sins no more! (see Jer. 31:34).

Finally, please understand that this indictment against us has "been nailed to the cross." In the ancient world, when a statement of debt was cancelled, it was nailed on a door for all to see. For Christians, our sins have been nailed to the cross of Christ and crucified with Him. Our debts were paid for in His death for our sins. The Lord has destroyed our sins once and forever on Calvary. Luther says that we must stop focusing on our sins, and instead remember the grace and mercy of God, that "Christ on the cross takes your sin from you, bears it for you, and destroys it." (LW 42:105). Our sins have been "swallowed up" in Christ. "He also takes your sins upon himself and overcomes them with his righteousness out of sheer mercy, and if you believe that, your sins will never work you harm." (Ibid.)

When we are dying we must remember that Christ has forgiven our sins once and for all on the cross of Calvary. Our sins have been cancelled, our slate has been wiped clean, and God has removed our guilt forever. Let us take faith in the work of Jesus Christ on our behalf, and never dishonor Him by lack of trust in His act of forgiving us. We need not take to our death the burden of our sins; we need to remember that Jesus, our Lord and Savior, has been punished for them, once and forever, and they are blotted out for all time.

Dear Lord, we thank you for the promises you make to us. Help us remember that our confessed sins have been removed from us and placed on your Son. Thank you for canceling our debt. We praise you for your grace to us, in Jesus Name, amen.

4
OUR FOCUS

"If then you have been raised with Christ, seek the things that are above, where Christ is, seated at the right hand of God. Set your minds on things that are above, not on things that are on earth."
Col. 3:1-2

When we are preparing for death we can sometimes become occupied with "things we have left undone" instead of the things of our future. This Word inspires us to change our orientation from this world to the next. It is of great benefit at any time in our lives, but especially as we prepare to go to be with the Lord.

Paul says "If you have been raised with Christ, seek the things that are above, where Christ is, seated at the right hand of God." In baptism we die and rise again with Christ into a new life of obedience to Him. As Christians we are not called to simply stop functioning in the world, but we are called to weigh everything in light of our eternal priority. We live to please Christ here, that He might be pleased with us when we get to heaven. Augustine would say that "we are no longer called to use God to enjoy the world, but to use the world in order to enjoy God forever." (City of God). This shift of priority is a necessary part of the Christian life, and a wonderful, positive way to prepare for death.

Paul says: "Set your minds on things that are above, not on things that are on earth." This plain command is easy to understand, but hard to put into practice. It is hard to let go of earthly priorities; whether family, work, or life goals. Yet, when we see our world in light of eternity, we can replace our worldly attitudes with those of heavenly love, and actually be more of a blessing by prayer and encouragement than we ever were before.

Moreover, when we set our mind on things above, our focus will be less on our earthly death and more on our heavenly life. Indeed, Luther tells Christians to think of death while they are living, but when they are dying, to meditate upon life. (LW 42:102). In the hour of our death our focus should be on eternal life, which has been given to us as a gift by our Lord.

Dear Lord, help us in the hour of our death, to focus on your priorities, the priorities of heaven. Help us concentrate on eternal life instead of earthly death, that we might revel in your victory on our behalf, and be ready for you when you come to take us home, we pray in Jesus Name, amen.

5
DEALING WITH PAIN

"For I consider that the sufferings of this present time are not worth comparing with the glory that is to be revealed to us."
Romans 8:18

One of the hardest challenges we face during our preparation for death is to keep our focus on heaven while we suffer on earth. This passage helps us to concentrate upon heaven even in the midst of our suffering.

What Paul does here is give us a comparison to meditate upon. He says "For I consider that the sufferings of this present time are not worth comparing to the glory that is to be revealed to us." Note here two truths: First, Paul does not deny the fact that this life is a vale of tears, which contains pain and discomfort. As our mortal body deteriorates we suffer under many sundry ailments, some painful to others, like dementia, and others painful to ourselves, like cancer. Paul does not discount the seriousness of the sufferings that we experience in this life.

How then can we cope with the sufferings of this life? The second thing Paul says is that we must deal with earthly sufferings, by "considering", "calculating, or weighing" them in comparison to the greatness of our future glory. Earthly suffering is the pathway through which we experience heavenly glory. Paul understood that the mortal body must die before it can be raised immortal. In I Corinthians 15 (a chapter well worth meditation), he says "What is sown is perishable, what is raised is perishable. It is sown in dishonor; it is raised in glory. It is sown in weakness; it is raised in power. It is sown a natural body; it is raised a spiritual body."

Our earthly body must die before we can be clothed with our heavenly body. The suffering of the present is going to lead us to a time and place in which we will no longer bear the image of the "man of dust", but shall "bear the image of the man of heaven" (Rom. 8:49).

We will be able to bear up under our earthly sufferings if we can keep our focus on our heavenly blessings. In this case, let us remember that our suffering is a pathway to the death of our bodies, not our souls, and that our souls are going to be clothed again in our *immortal, heavenly bodies*, which will be like those of our Lord Jesus Christ. "This perishable body must put on the imperishable, and this mortal body must put on immortality." (Rom. 15:53).

Dear Lord, we pray that you would keep our focus on heaven, that we might triumph over the sufferings we experience on earth. Thank you for the promise of a new, heavenly body, made in the image of your Son. We look forward to the day in which we will turn in the mortal for that which is immortal. In Jesus Name, amen.

6

ENCOURAGEMENT

*"So we do not lose heart. Though our outer nature is wasting
away, our inner nature is being renewed day by day."*
2 Corinthians 4:16

It is true that if we depended on the Lord for this life alone
we truly have reason to be miserable. This is not the case at all.
The Lord has promised us life after death in a body which is
like his glorious resurrection body. We have a hope for a future
life with Jesus and our loved ones, in a mansion in the heavens.
Since we believe that the same Lord who raised Jesus "will raise
us also with Jesus and bring us" (2 Cor. 6:14) we can conquer
discouragement. We can say with Paul "we do not lose heart."

Two things are happening to us simultaneously. First, "our
outer nature is wasting away." The Lord does not deny the
fact that our outer man decays, weakens, and dies. Our bodies
are subject to deterioration and failure. This is a fact which
we often postpone accepting throughout our adult lives. The
reason why so many people struggle horribly with end of life
issues is that they refuse to face death while they are living,
but try to live in denial of its reality. We Christians are taught
by the Lord to deal with our deaths early, that we can spend
the end of our lives on earth preparing for our wonderful
future with the Lord in glory.

The second thing that is happening to us is that "our inner
nature is being renewed day by day." This is a reality only in

Christians, as the Holy Spirit lives within us, feeding our spiritual life with comfort, truth, and strength. Our inner nature is Christ's eternal life living within us *now*, by the power of the Holy Spirit. As we read God's Word, pray, worship, and love in His name, God is at work in us to give us growth and maturity in our inner nature. You can see God's work in the radiant saints who lay on their deathbed giving out blessing to others, and being at peace despite their circumstances. Let us seek the Lord ourselves, that we might never lose heart in our sufferings, but submit to the two realities that we are experiencing. When we are weak physically, we can indeed be strong spiritually.

Dear Lord, we pray that you would help us see what you are doing in our lives, that we would not grieve the death of our bodies, but rejoice in the renewal of our souls. Thank you for working in us. In Jesus Name, amen.

7
AFFLICTIONS LEAD TO GLORY

"For this slight momentary affliction is preparing for us
An eternal weight of glory beyond all comparison, as we look not to the
things that are seen but to the things that are unseen. For the things that
are seen are transient, but the things that are unseen are eternal."
2 Cor. 4:17–18

When we first read this verse we can become angry, thinking that Paul is somehow discounting the length and breadth of what we suffer before we die. This is hardly the case (see 4:8ff. and 11:23ff). What Paul is doing here is repeating what he wrote in Romans 8:18: He is contrasting temporal suffering with eternal blessing. He says that our temporary suffering cannot be compared with life without pain, sorrow, tears, or affliction. We get that future life in glory, and we keep it forever. Our present afflictions are transient, in that they have a beginning and an end in time. Therefore they carry much less weight for us than the blessings of glory, which last throughout eternity.

Moreover, he says that our present affliction "is preparing for us an eternal weight of glory beyond all comparison." Our suffering on earth contributes in some way to our preparation for heaven. Our suffering is certainly not the cause of our reward in heaven, but it certainly does work together for good to those who have been called by God (Rom. 8:28). As the pain of childbirth recedes once a child is born, so the afflictions of the sufferer in this life will be forgotten in the boundless joy of eternal life.

As we prepare to die, our focus must change from temporal life to eternal life. Paul says "as we look not to the things that are seen but to the things that are unseen." We have to set our minds on things that God has promised to us in His Word, and ask Him to grant us the faith to trust Him for what is future.

What we do not see now is far more important than what we can observe with our eyes. What we can see is pain, disease, and death. What is unseen now is life behind the door of physical death. We must have faith to submit to walking through that door to the future, *our future in the presence of the Lord.*

Let us note that Paul says that this "weight of glory" is "beyond all comparison." We must take God at His Word.

In I Corinthians 2:9 Paul writes: 'What no eye has seen, nor ear heard, nor the heart of man imagined, what God has prepared for those who love him."

Our future is bright and full of wonders that are indescribable. We go to that future by the grace of God, through faith in Jesus Christ as Lord and Savior. We have no reason to fear that which is unseen, because we are in the hands of the Sovereign King of the Universe, who loves us, and has given us hope through the resurrection of His Son, our Savior, Jesus Christ.

Dear Lord, give us the faith to look forward from this hard time to eternity. Grant us a vision of Glory today, we pray in Jesus Name, amen.

8

OUR NEW HOME

*"For we know that if the tent, which is our earthly home, is destroyed, we have
a building from God, a house not made with hands, eternal in the heavens."*
2 Cor. 5:1

In this text we find one of the greatest promises to be
found in Scripture. God has promised that after the death of
our physical bodies, we will be given new, spiritual bodies.
"For we know that if the tent, which is our earthly home, is
destroyed, we have a building from God." This truth should
eliminate our fear of death, and inspire our eager expectation
of good things to come.

Why should we be excited about the change of one body
for another? Shouldn't we cherish the body we have lived in
all these years? Paul gives us three characteristics about our
"newer model" body which should make us excited about
receiving it. First, Paul says that our new home shall be a
'building from God.' The source of our new body is the Lord
our God, the creator of heaven and earth. The same God
who made the mountains, oceans, rivers and trees is going to
make a new body for us, in which our mortal body will put
on immortality. We will be like Jesus! Meditate on this reality,
and you will be greatly encouraged.

Secondly, Paul says that this body is "not made with
hands." The best of human workmanship suffers from
rust, deterioration, breakage, and destruction over time.

God has promised to replace our old, deteriorated, broken bodies with bodies "not made with hands." We will be transformed from "a man of dust" to "bear the image of the man of heaven." This new body, not made with hands, is imperishable, and will never fall apart, get sick, suffer, or die. What a promise!

Thirdly, Paul says that this new body is "eternal in the heavens." This new body will not be made in Detroit, but in heaven. It will not be made to fall apart over time, but will last throughout eternity. This is a great promise which is to be fulfilled in our future. We have every reason to rejoice at the prospect of leaving this old shell behind, and receiving from God a beautiful, permanent replacement that shall never suffer again.

Dear Lord, we thank you for the promises which you make to us in your Word. Thank you for our new, eternal body, In Jesus Name, amen.

9
LIFE OVER MORTALITY

*"For in this tent we groan, longing to put on our heavenly dwelling,
if indeed by putting it on we may not be found naked. For while we
are still in this tent, we groan, being burdened-not that we would be
unclothed, but that we would be further clothed, so that what is mortal
may be swallowed up by life. He who prepared us for this very thing is
God, who has given us the Spirit as a guarantee."*
2 Cor. 5:2-5

Believers have another perspective than those without Christ.
We believe that there is more to life beyond this earthly existence,
and there is something beyond our physical death which is a joy
beyond words. The unbeliever groans during the suffering of death
for many reasons, one of which is the desire to stay alive on this
earth. Paul says that Christians groan during earthly trial because we
desire a better life, the life with God, beyond this earthly existence.
Christians have a longing to turn in the old body of death for the
"heavenly dwelling" that God has promised us.

None of us want to become a naked soul, removed from
our earthly bodies. We, like every person, would prefer not to
have our clothes stripped from us. The wonderful reality for
us is that we receive new clothes in place of those which have
been removed. Calvin argues that none of us would mind
throwing away old clothes if they can be replaced with "better
garments" (Inst. 10:68). When it comes to death, we Christians
have an entirely different belief than our non-Christian loved

ones. We look forward to leaving our old bodies and receiving new, immortal bodies, made by God, eternal in the heavens.

God has promised that in the future "what is mortal shall be swallowed up by life." The earthly body we live in now is corruptible, mutable and mortal. We experience this reality every day as we grow older, and begin to weaken. No matter how hard we fight it, our bodies age, eventually deteriorate, and die. This reality is part of the fabric of earthly existence. It is this mortal body of earth which God will transform into a new, imperishable, incorruptible, eternal body. The greatest character of this new body is that it is not subject to death, but is imbued with "life."

Finally, let us note who the guarantor of this promise is: "He who has prepared us for this very thing is God, who has given us the Spirit as a guarantee." God did not create us to be mortal and die. He created us to live with Him in eternal bliss in the Garden, without want, worry or pain. Mortality is a consequence of the fall, and a terrible blight on the landscape of creation. God has promised us that He is preparing us to assume the position we were created to assume, that of people made in the image of God, living without sin and death. He is preparing us to take our place as the pinnacle of his created beings, and is going to restore us to that state of being. The Holy Spirit lives in us in order to move us to this place of honor and blessing. His presence is a guarantee that God is at work in us to prepare us to walk through the door of physical death to a new life that is beyond our wildest dreams. We will be fully blessed when we receive our glorified bodies, which God will grant to us on that great day.

Dear Lord, we thank you so much for the promises you have made to us. Please help us remember them now, in this time of difficulty. We indeed groan, in hope of better days with you in heaven. In Jesus Name, amen.

10

OUR CHRISTIAN DUTY

"Yes, we are of good courage, and would rather be away from the body and at home with the Lord. So whether we are at home or away, we make it our aim to please him. For we must all appear before the judgment seat of Christ, so that each one may receive what is due for what he has done in the body, whether good or evil."
2 Cor. 5:8-10

This passage contains several important truths which we should take to heart. Paul here speaks of matters of personal preferences, and important goals for our lives, as well as gives us serious information concerning the future.

First, Paul gives us his personal preference: "we would rather be away from the body and at home with the Lord." This was his choice, the product of much maturity and meditation on eternal truth. He had lived his life of service for the Lord. He had worked for the Lord for many years, and desired to see him again, face to face. He was attached to his heavenly home with Jesus before he left earth. This preference is something which we can develop as we walk with the Lord on this earth. As we get to know and trust Him more, we gradually realize that we have more affinity with heaven than with earth. Do not be surprised that you experience this as well as you prepare to die. There is a time to cling to life, and a time to long for death. There is a time to prefer go to be with the Lord than stay in a hospital bed. This preference is of our own volition, and is decided gradually as we grow in maturity.

Secondly, Paul gives us an important personal goal. He says: "So whether we are at home or away, we make it our aim to please him." We are not in charge of the time of our death. We are, however, in charge of the way we lead our lives in preparation for death. Paul says that no matter whether he lived or died, he would make it his goal to please the Lord. The time of death can be a very selfish time in the life of people. Yet the Apostle would have us seek to serve the Lord even while we are dying. We can be a source of blessing to others even on our death-beds. We can, like Jacob and others, bless our loved ones with words they will remember forever. The last prayers we make with our families will be what they will hold in their hearts forever. Let us make it our aim to please the Lord in whatever circumstance we find ourselves.

Why is this important? Paul tells us that "we must all appear before the judgment seat of Christ, so that each one may receive what is due for what he has done in the body, whether good or evil." We are accountable to God for what we do while we live on this earth. We should make it our goal to please the Lord every day we have on this earth, for we are promised that we will give account for how we have spent these precious days. We are called to live while dying, because as long as we are here, there may be an opportunity to serve our Lord by loving others as He would have them loved. May God help us fulfill our ministry here, that we might receive reward in our heavenly home.

Dear Lord, help us live this life with the aim of pleasing you in every way. Help us see every day you give us as an opportunity to love and bless our loved ones. Help us not be selfish, but accept the lot we find ourselves in today. May we bear fruit for you continually, until you take us to our home in heaven, we pray in Jesus Name, amen.

II

WORK IS FINITE

"We must work the works of him who sent me while it is day; night is coming, when no one can work."
John 9:4

The one thing that terminal illness does, is that it brings to our attention the fact that life on this earth is limited and finite. Jesus our Lord and Savior recognized this reality during His earthly ministry. There indeed is a time for every season under heaven. There is a time to work, and a time when no work can take place. Jesus accomplished an incredible amount of work in a very few years of public ministry. He did His work with a great deal of urgency and energy, because He understood the time was short. He knew that He would be on the earth as its inspiring light for only a certain period of time, and He performed miracles in light of that reality.

Note that in this passage Jesus says "*We* must work." He includes His disciples in the work that must be done. He includes us in the ministry of work here as He did in the ministry of teaching and witness in John 3:11. Why is this important? We are called by our Lord Jesus to work, witness, and testify to the truth with Him during our time on this earth.

This time of witness has a terminus. Jesus says: "night is coming, when no one can work." We cannot and must not live as if we can postpone our labor on behalf of the Lord.

We do not know the day or hour when our life on earth will be completed. While it is day, we must do the things God has called us to do, for there will come a time very soon when we are unable to do them.

Paul says that "we are created in Christ Jesus for good works, which God prepared beforehand, that we should walk in them." (Eph. 2:10) The knowledge of our immanent death should give us a stirring in our conscience to complete the works which God has given us to do on this earth. This is one of the reasons why many Christians receive a burst of adrenalin after processing the news that they have only a short time to live. God gives great energy to his saints before death, that they might be able to finish certain works of love before they go home to heaven.

Dear Lord, I thank you for showing me that there is an end to earthly labor. Please give me your grace in order that I might complete my work for you before you call me home, in Jesus Name, amen.

12

CHANGING CLOTHES

"Besides this you know the time, that the hour has come for you to wake
from sleep. For salvation is nearer to us now than when we first believed.
The night is far gone; the day is at hand. So then let us cast off the works
of darkness and put on the armor of light…But put on the Lord Jesus
Christ, and make no provision for the flesh, to gratify its desires."
Romans 13:11-12,14

This text speaks of three things which we must do as we
seriously prepare to meet the Lord. First, we must wake up from
our sleep. Paul writes: "the hour has come for you to wake from
sleep." Indeed, when we first hear news of impending death, we
can become depressed and lethargic, not wanting to move or
do anything. Depression can produce inertia and fatigue, which
inspires sleep, not action. Yet Paul gives us a rationale for waking
up: the reality that "salvation is nearer now." When we realize
that our days on earth are moving on quickly, we realize that we
have little time to waste on sleep and depression, but must make
the most of the days we have left.

Secondly, Paul tells us to get rid of those things which weigh
us down, and keep us from making the most of our time.
He says "let us cast off the works of darkness and put on the
armor of light." We may have lived our life with a lot of selfish
priorities and pleasures. When we are preparing to die these
pleasures and pastimes are seen for what they truly are, an
incredible waste of precious time! Now we must drop them all

away, and concentrate our remaining energy on things which please the Lord, not the flesh.

Thirdly, Paul tells us to "put on the Lord Jesus Christ, and make no provision for the flesh, to gratify its desires." It is time that we recognize Jesus as our priority, and seek to serve Him without distraction. We must "put on Jesus Christ", His words and His call, His love and His servant's heart, His kindness and His sacrifice, asking Him to control all of our actions, conforming them to His perfect example. We must clothe ourselves with Jesus, not the fashions of the flesh.

If we wake up, and drop off all the weight of selfishness, and make Jesus the one priority of our remaining days on this earth, we will please Him, and best prepare for death.

Dear Lord, thank you for reminding me to keep working for you. Help me lay aside all selfishness, and serve you with all the energy I have left, in Jesus Name, amen.

13
DILIGENCE

"For this very reason, make every effort to supplement your faith with virtue, and virtue with knowledge, and knowledge with self-control, and self-control with steadfastness, and steadfastness with godliness, and godliness with brotherly affection, and brotherly affection with love. For if these qualities are yours and are increasing, they keep you from being ineffective or unfruitful in the knowledge of our Lord Jesus Christ."
2 Peter 1:5-8

If there is one time in our life that we want to be the best we can be, it is during the time that we are preparing to die. We want to please the Lord, and bless those around us. These words of Peter should inspire us to the characteristics which we should cultivate at this time.

Virtue is moral goodness and excellence. We want to truly act in a way that makes others see Christ in us.

Knowledge is the accumulation of spiritual truth. The knowledge of what the Scripture teaches concerning life and death is of paramount importance to our whole life as Christians, but gives great comfort at the time of our death.

Self-control can be quite difficult during times of great stress, as during illness and grief. Yet, if we place the Lord forefront in our hearts, our emotions can be kept from ruling our actions, and what we say can be of great benefit to others.

Steadfastness is a steady calm during the storms of life. We must take God at His Word, and hold to the promises He makes to us, especially at times of affliction. The Lord's Word can calm our hearts, and give us great peace in spite of our circumstances.

Godliness is much greater a virtue than manliness. The Lord wants us to display His likeness to those around us, that they might be drawn to Him through us.

Brotherly affection is a marvelous quality for us to exhibit before death. Those we love will grieve our passing away, and can use our affection now while we can still show it. Letters, phone calls, e-mails, and visits from us have a great influence over how our families deal with our leaving them.

Love is the greatest quality which we can exhibit to others and to God. When we express our love for our loved ones, we prepare them to let us go, and give them memories to cling to far after we have gone to heaven.

These qualities of virtue, knowledge, self-control, steadfastness, godliness, brotherly affection, and love should be sought after with all our hearts, that we might truly be effective witnesses for Christ to those we love, and prepare them to let us go.

Dear Lord, let me not give up seeking for these values that you have called me to exhibit to those I love. May people see Christ in me, even at this difficult time in my life, I pray in Jesus Name, amen.

14

BE WHO WE ARE

"Therefore, brothers, be all the more diligent to make your calling and election sure, for if you practice these qualities you will never fall. For in this way there will be richly provided for you an entrance into the eternal kingdom of our Lord and Savior Jesus Christ."
2 Peter 1:10-11

The Lord wants us to exhibit in our lives the fruit of our salvation, in not only the good works which the Lord has ordained for us to do, but also the virtues which reflect His image in us.

We confirm our election as we bear fruit for Jesus Christ. Moreover, we can stand against all failures of faith by seeking to cultivate the qualities that honor our Lord. Peter says: "for if you practice these qualities you will never fall." It is God who by grace inspires us to live lives which honor and glorify His name. It is God who sets these ideals before us, and enables us to practice them. The Holy Spirit in us convicts our hearts, moving us to value and exhibit the qualities that please God. As we surrender to Him, He works in us.

These qualities can grow more and more in us, until we at last are granted an entrance into the Kingdom of our Lord and Savior. The same Lord who saved us is by grace is conforming us into the image of His Son, and preparing us an entrance into His presence. As we yield to His guidance in our lives, we move forward, adding one virtue upon another, until we stand directly before the Lord in glory. Our sanctification is a cooperative effort, in which God supplies, and we submit to the grace of virtue. He has called us to seek to add to our faith certain qualities, which conform us into His image, and prepare us to enter the gates of heaven. Peter says "For in this way there will be richly provided for you an entrance into the eternal kingdom of our Lord and Savior Jesus Christ."

God has provided for us all things which pertain to life and godliness. As we receive His grace, day by day, and seek to conform into His image, He leads us inexorably forward toward heaven, to which He alone can provide entrance. This God has promised to do for us, praise His holy name!

Dear Lord, forgive me for ever forgetting for a moment what you have done to save me. Help me every day to seek to add to my faith the virtues which honor you, and enable me by your grace to be the person you have called me to be, In Jesus Name, amen.

15
GIVING TO CHRIST

"'Come, you who are blessed by my Father, inherit the kingdom prepared for you from the foundation of the world. For I was hungry and you gave me food, I was thirsty and you gave me drink, I was a stranger and you welcomed me, I was naked and you clothed me, I was sick and you visited me, I was in prison and you came to me.' Then the righteous will answer him, saying, 'Lord, when did we see you hungry and feed you, or thirsty and give you drink? And when did we see you a stranger and welcome you, or naked and clothe you? And when did we see you sick or in prison and visit you?' And the King will answer them, 'Truly, I say to you, as you did it to one of the least of these my brothers, you did it to me.'"
Mt. 25:34-40

This extensive quote is of the highest significance for us as we prepare to die. Jesus here separates the 'sheep from the goats', and identifies those who will inherit the kingdom of heaven. He makes it clear that a Christian evidences his or her love for Him by their actions towards others. We serve Jesus by serving each other. Jesus fully expects us to evidence our faith in Him by the acts we perform in our daily lives. Our acts by no means save us, but they identify us as Christians. A person who claims to be a Christian without evidencing love for their neighbor is deluding themselves. Jesus convicts us to love Him by loving each other. In his first Epistle, John writes: "We know that we have passed out of death into life, because we love the brothers." (I Jn. 3:14)

Our love for each other is shown in concrete deeds of kindness, from sharing our food, drink, shelter, clothing, time and talents with each other, to visiting each other in our various needs. These are marks of genuine discipleship to Jesus Christ. They are so foundational to our identity as Christians that Jesus uses them as a criterion by which he judges all humankind. These acts of obedience do not save us, but are organically connected to our faith, as fruit is to the tree that bears it.

Let us make every effort to use the time we have left on this earth in a way which pleases our Lord, and gives concrete evidence to our relationship with Him. The things we do on this earth matter to God, and to us, as well as those in need.

Dear Lord, thank you for reminding us that our faith must evidence itself in works of love to others. Give us the strength to bless someone today, in Jesus Name, amen.

16
Forgiving others

"If one has a complaint against another, forgiving each other, as the Lord has forgiven you, so you also must forgive."
Col. 3:13

There will be days during your final illness that you are simply unable to go anywhere or even leave your bedroom. It is during these times that you can serve the Lord in very quiet, but important ways. The Lord who sees your heart will be very pleased with you as you obey His Word.

One of the most important things we ever do as Christians is to release others from the resentment we can hold against them. During the course of our earthly life there have been people who have injured us by their words and deeds. We all have someone somewhere who we have a legitimate complaint against. Paul says that as Christians we are called to forgive each other. This exhortation can be followed on our sickbed, as we write or call, or pray in obedience to this command.

Our forgiveness of those who have wronged us is not contingent on a change in their behavior, or their repentance; it is based upon our own experience of God's forgiveness in our own lives. We must remember what God has done for us in sending His Son to calvary to die for our sins, to forgive *our* trespasses, and then act in kind to those who have sinned against us.

Our forgiveness of others is not optional. Paul says that we "must" forgive. Here he only echoes our Lord Jesus, who in the Sermon on the Mount states: "For if you forgive others their trespasses, your heavenly Father will also forgive you, but if you do not forgive others their trespasses, neither will your Father forgive your trespasses." (Mt. 6:14-15)

When we release others from our judgment, we free them to come under conviction to repent of their actions.

Some of us have been deeply hurt by others, and find this Scripture hard to obey. Yet, it is a sign of our Christian faith that must be evidenced in our lives. Let go of all grudges out of obedience to God. Remember all of your sins long enough to run to God in prayer, asking Him to help you treat others as you would have Him treat you. Then you can have great peace as you wait for God to take you home.

Dear Lord, we forgive those who up to now we have held a grudge against. Forgive us for not seeing ourselves as you do, in Jesus Name, amen.

17

PRAYER

"The prayer of a righteous person has great power as it is working."
James 5:16

Another thing that we can do to occupy our time during our last illness is to pray. This action, by which we speak to God on behalf of others and ourselves, is one of the greatest privileges we have as Christians. It is easy to be distracted by illness, by the medical professionals who try to help us, and the suffering of pain itself. These distractions must recede over time to give us time to quietly wait for God to come for us and take us home. As we begin to let go of this world, it is a blessing to be able to strengthen the bridge between heaven and earth by prayer. Moreover, there are many things that need prayer during this time. It is important therefore, that we take God at His Word and trust what He says about prayer: "the prayer of a righteous person has great power."

Elijah was a person just like us, but he prayed that it would not rain, and God answered his request. We are just like Elijah, in that we own no righteousness except that which comes to us as a gift through Jesus Christ our Lord. He is our righteousness (I Cor. 1:30). The Lord has given us the tremendous privilege of prayer, and He has promised that He will hear and answer petitions which are in accordance with His will. In our physical weakness, we can be strong in the Lord and in the strength of *His might*. Our prayers can have great power for good, and benefit all around us.

What then should we pray for as we prepare to die? We should pray for our families, that God would comfort them, protect them, guide them, and grant them faith in Him during this time of pain and suffering. We should pray for those who are also suffering end of life sicknesses outside the blessing of faith in the Lord, that they might come to know Him as their Lord and Savior. We should pray for all those we love who do not know the Lord, that they would not die without Him. We should pray especially for our spouses, that they might be comforted as they grieve our loss with the comfort of the Holy Spirit. We should pray for all the children in our families, that they might be blessed and led by the Lord all the days of their lives. We should pray for those around the world who are suffering under deprivation, persecution, or sickness, that God would meet all their needs according to His riches in glory in Christ Jesus. And, we should pray for ourselves, that we would be faithful even unto death. There is much, much more we can pray for, but these thoughts can serve as a springboard to fruitful hours of intercession, for which God will bless you both on earth and in heaven.

Dear Lord, grant to me the commitment to pray each day that I am on this earth. Use me to bless my loved ones and you. Thank you for allowing me this privilege. Bring to my heart those who need to be prayed for today, I pray in Jesus Name, amen.

18

LOVE

"The end of all things is at hand; therefore be self-controlled and sober-minded for the sake of your prayers. Above all, keep loving one another earnestly, since love covers a multitude of sins."

I Peter 4:7-8

We Christians are called to have an entirely different attitude toward impending death than others. We are not to be like the characters in Boccaccio's *Decameron*, who ran from the plague to a hideaway where they could indulge in selfish pleasure until they died. We are called to be sober and serious during times of crisis, in order to be properly prepared to pray and intercede on behalf of the dying.

More than this, we are called by God to "keep loving one another earnestly." When over one-third of Europe died in the period of the plague (cir. 1349), there were many people who abandoned family and neighbors during their time of need, out of fear of catching the plague from assisting others. By great contrast, there were courageous Christian workers, like the nuns around Strasbourg, who gave their lives giving aid, comfort, and succor to those who contracted that terrible disease. We too are called by God to be a source of comfort at all times, whether in war, illness, or accident.

It is hard to face terminal illness. We sometimes are tempted to withdraw into ourselves, and not communicate with those around us. God would have us continue to love each other in every circumstance we find ourselves in, whether pleasant or difficult.

Why should we "keep loving earnestly"? Peter says that "love covers a multitude of sins." In this Peter quotes Proverbs 10:12, which states "hatred stirs up strife, but love covers all offenses." Offenses are covered over by the avalanche of loving deeds. Loving acts bury sins by forgiveness. This is a great and wonderful characteristic of love. Love does not save us, but it makes our world better and more beautiful by its presence. Hate disappears where love reigns supreme.

Dear Lord, help me to love at all times, no matter what circumstance I find myself in. Help me to cover offenses with kindnesses, that the world around me would be better because I have lived here, in Jesus Name, amen.

19

THAT ONE SIN

"If we confess our sins, he is faithful and just to forgive us our sins and to cleanse us from all unrighteousness."
I John 1:9

Guilt is difficult during any time of our lives, but during the period before our death, its pain can become quite acute. We remember the course of our lives and choose to dwell on our failures instead of our successes. Sometimes, one failure in particular will plague us, and because we cannot forgive ourselves for it, we assume that God cannot or will not forgive it either. This guilt is multiplied if it involves sin against someone we love. We wonder about whether they and God have forgiven us, even though we may have asked forgiveness of them many years ago. To remedy this situation, we have to take God at His Word and obey what it says. I John 1:9 says: "If we confess our sins, he is faithful and just to forgive us our sins and to cleanse us from all unrighteousness."

So, let us confess our fault to the Lord, repenting of our actions and asking His forgiveness.

Secondly, let us depend not upon our feelings (which are suspect at best), but on the character of God, who loves us and is faithful to the promises of His Word. For us to doubt that God would forgive our confessed sin is to say that God is a liar, which He certainly is not. It is a dishonor for us not to take God at His Word, for He has never broken a promise and never will. God is not like us; He is faithful to His promises. Therefore, let us trust Him to do what He has promised to do. Remember also that God is just. Our sins have been properly punished by Him. Jesus "was wounded for our transgressions; he was crushed for our iniquities, upon him was the chastisement that brought us peace....the Lord has laid on him the iniquity of us all." (Isaiah 53:5,6b) The Lord's justice has been meted out, once and forever, on the spotless lamb of God, who came to take away the sin of the world (John 1:29). He has taken our sins away from us, removing them completely. We must trust in His finished work on the cross of calvary; anything less dishonors Him.

He has promised to "cleanse us from all unrighteousness." We are washed with His precious blood, shed for us. Instead of condemning ourselves (an act of self-loathing which is not helpful), let us now therefore rejoice in the Lord, and humbly thank Him for His wonderful, matchless grace to us. Let us remember the words of Paul when he wrote: "There is therefore now no condemnation for those who are in Christ Jesus." (Romans 8:1) Let us take God at His Word, and rejoice that we are forgiven, now and forever.

Dear Lord, bless this truth to our hearts, that we might obey it faithfully whenever we fail you. Forgive us for ever believing that our sins cannot be forgiven. Help those who we have sinned against to forgive us, as you have forgiven both of us, we pray in Christ's Name, amen.

20

SHARING WITH OTHERS

"Sell your possessions, and give to the needy. Provide yourselves with
moneybags that do not grow old, with a treasure in the heavens that
does not fail, where no thief approaches and no moth destroys. For where
your treasure is, there will your heart be also."
Luke 12:33-34

It is often said that 'you can't take it with you', as if it were
completely true. For those in the world, whose possessions
are their fortune, this is surely the case. Christians, however,
are given other counsel. Yes, we are told by Jesus to "sell
our possessions and give to the poor". This divestiture is a
blessing for them, and for us. The Lord makes an account
of our generosity here, and deposits our wealth in heaven,
where what we have is kept theft-proof and moth-proof
(see I Peter 1:3-4).

The Lord makes it clear that acts of love and kindness in
this life pay great dividends in the next. What we do on
behalf of 'the least of the brethren' Jesus considers to be given
to Him. He is pleased when we divest ourselves of earthly
wealth in His Name and for His sake. This is a wonderful,
positive thing to do as we prepare to die. What we own now
another may need when we are gone. Let us, while we have
faculties to do so, will out our possessions, being generous
not only with those we love, but on those who are in need.
Our portfolios must not remain deposited in the Bank of

Earth, but in the Bank of Heaven. The Lord wants us to use our wealth here in a way that glorifies God in heaven.

In this life investments in stocks or bonds may be lost during market downturns, and economic recessions. In contrast, every investment we make in heaven is secure, and is not subject to prevailing earthly conditions. Therefore, the prudent investment for the Christian is indeed the Bank of Heaven, which secures our deposits by the Word and faithfulness of Almighty God, the maker of heaven and earth. Let us not cling to earthly wealth that cannot comfort us in eternity, but rather share God's bounty with the poor in our midst, pleasing Him, and meeting their needs.

Dear Lord, help me truly have a generous spirit, that I might never cling to wealth, but give away what I have to help those less fortunate than myself. Guide me in the use of the wealth you have given to me, that it might be spent out for your honor and glory, in Jesus Name, amen.

21

SEPARATION ANXIETY

"Who shall separate us from the love of Christ? Shall tribulation, or distress, or persecution, or famine, or nakedness, or danger, or sword? As it is written, 'for your sake we are being killed all the day long; we are regarded as sheep to be slaughtered.' No, in all these things we are more than conquerors through him who loved us. For I am sure that neither death nor life, nor angels nor rulers, nor things present nor things to come...nor anything else in all creation, will be able to separate us from the love of God in Christ Jesus our Lord."

Romans 8:35-39

This Scripture is one of the greatest words of comfort in all of the Word of God. It is very worthy of putting to memory, as it is the strongest antidote to that which we fear: separation. The Lord has told us here that no matter what our situation, He will never leave us to face it alone. We will never be separated from God's love for us. Our sickness, weakness, pain, and death are not outside the domain of our heavenly Father. Nothing, literally *nothing* can separate us from experiencing His love, which is there for us in all our extremities.

Christians are not "more than conquerors" over death because we are strong, but we obtain victory over the suffering of this life by the grace of God in Christ Jesus alone.

We therefore can be sure that "neither death nor life" "will be able to separate us from the love of God in Christ

Jesus our Lord." We have no reason to fear death, for the Lord has promised to be there to open death's door for us, so that we may enter into eternal life. This is the blessing of God to us; that we have victory over death through our Lord Jesus Christ.

Not only this, we can be sure that neither "things present nor things to come" "will be able to separate us from the love of God in Christ Jesus our Lord."

The suffering we may be undergoing at present may be severe, but it cannot keep us from the invincible love of Jesus for us, who comforts us in our affliction. We may have even more pain to experience in our future, but our Lord has promised that His love can pierce our most pitiful cry, and calm the tempest of our hearts. The Lord has promised us "I will never leave you nor forsake you" (Hebrews 13:5). Take Him at His Word. When you are facing the moment of your death, you will not be alone, because the Lord who loves you will be there for you, to hold you and keep you, comfort and caress you, and bring you safely through the door into bliss.

Dear Lord, I thank you for this glorious promise. Give me grace to take you at your Word. May your presence give me the courage I need to face the ordeal ahead, I pray in the Name of Jesus, amen.

22

SEPARATION

"Love never ends."
I Corinthians 1:8

One of the hardest trials we ever face is the prospect of separation from our loved ones at the time of our death. This reality causes much heartache for us and for our spouses and families. No matter who we are, we loom large in the life of someone, whether parent, child, husband, wife, or friend. We will be missed when we leave this earth for our home in heaven.

At this point we should take special notice of those who will miss us the most: our spouses. One of the hardest lectures I ever heard in seminary was the exposition of Matthew 22:30, in which Jesus said that "in the resurrection they neither marry nor are given in marriage, but are like angels in heaven." Marriage is an earthly blessing, which does not continue in eternity. Our bodies change to be more like angels than people on earth. Our relationships are transformed into less of a physical, and more of a spiritual character. This is a truth that we must not ignore.

How can we cope with the reality that our marriages dissolve at death? For one thing, our spouse is freed after our death to marry another person who loves the Lord (I Corinthians 7:39). This is a good thing, which can give them great comfort, especially if we die while they are fairly young.

More importantly, we should remember and take comfort in the statement Paul makes to us in our text. "Love never ends." Relationships can change through death, but our love for each other is absolutely indissoluble. Love is an eternal verity, unlike other gifts of the Spirit. Our love for each other will be taken through our death and survive intact for all eternity. This is something precious. We love our families, and cherish them. We will continue to love and cherish them for eternity, in glory with the Lord. How this blessing will translate in heaven is beyond our comprehension, but we know that our Christian love is not a finite thing, but an eternal gift, which lasts forever.

This is a Scripture that we should read to our loved ones before we die, so they know that we will never stop loving them, in time or in eternity. This should comfort their hearts, as it comforts our own.

Dear Lord, we thank you that love transcends time and eternity. Thank you so much for the relationships you have blessed us with in this life. Help us to so bless our loved ones here, that they might be prepared to let us go, in Jesus Name, amen.

23
A FOOT IN TWO CAMPS

"For to me to live is Christ, and to die is gain. If I am to live in the flesh, that means fruitful labor for me. Yet which I shall choose I cannot tell. I am hard pressed between the two. My desire is to depart and be with Christ, for that is far better. But to remain in the body is more necessary on your account."
Phil. 1:21-24

There will come a time during our trial with death that we will come to the conclusion that a new, immortal body, the presence of the Lord and our departed loved ones, and the end of all pain have become more attractive to us than staying on this earth. Paul was not terminally ill when he wrote these words to us, but he had come to the conclusion that he wanted heaven more than life on earth, eternity more than time.

He said "For me to live is Christ, and to die is gain." Earthly life meant service to Christ who lived in him. Death was the blessing of heavenly reward and infinite fellowship with his Lord and Savior.

Paul contrasted his life of earthly labor with the blessing of eternal life, and opted in favor of the latter. Yet, as he said, he was "hard pressed between the two." Why? He knew what a hardship his leaving would mean to those who depended upon him.

Paul had a foot in both camps, earth and heaven, loved ones on earth and the face of God in heaven. We too will come to a place in our journey when we are of two opinions regarding living or dying. Fortunately, we are not forced to make the final decision, as the Lord will take us in His time, when it is best for all concerned.

Yet, this position between our family on earth and our brethren in heaven is a real dilemma, which we will experience. Let us just remember that God knows what is best for us, and trust Him to bring us to a place of submission to His sovereign will, come life or death.

Dear Lord, thank you for letting us live on earth today for the sake of our loved ones. We know that heaven is better than suffering on earth, but we cling to the people who are precious to us here. Prepare them and us for the day you take us home. We love you, and trust you to take us when it is your time, in Jesus Name, amen.

24

NO MORE TEARS

"He will wipe away every tear from their eyes, and death shall be no more, neither shall there be mourning nor crying nor pain anymore, for the former things have passed away."
Revelation 21:4

There is coming a time in the future that Christians shall experience a tremendous change of venue and lifestyle. After the judgment, our Lord is going to create a new heaven and a new earth in place of the old. He is then going to live in the new Jerusalem in intimate fellowship with us. He has promised us that specific changes will take place, which will make our lives joyous and blessed. What are these wonderful changes that our Lord will make?

First, God has promised that 'death shall be no more'. We all hate death, and the specter of gloom it brings into our lives. There will be a time when death dies forever, in which we will neither experience the death of the body or the soul, but shall live eternally, like angels in the heavens. This is a reason to be hopeful about the future.

Secondly, God has promised that there will be an end to all "mourning." We have known the sorrow of grief. It is exhausting, depressing and debilitating at times. The Lord has promised that we will experience a time in which mourning will be a thing of the distant past, which will end forever. Isn't that wonderful?

Thirdly, God has promised that there will be a time that there will no longer be any "crying", (except perhaps for joy!) We have cried on earth as we have experienced the pain of sorrow, sickness, and loss of loved ones. This will end, thank God!

Fourthly, God has promised that there will be a time when we will not experience "pain" anymore. Who of us would not like to live forever without pain? That is what God has promised to those who love Him.

This is what we have to look forward to in heaven with the Lord. This is why we should be excited about "going home" to where Jesus is, seated at the right hand of the Father.

We not only have every reason not to fear death, we have every reason to declare it defeated by the victory of our Lord Jesus Christ (I Cor. 15:57).

As we prepare for death, let us remember again the counsel of Luther, who told us to look at death while we are living, so that when we are dying, we can meditate on life! Meditate upon your life in heaven, and you will certainly gain the victory over your short life on earth.

Dear Lord, we thank you for the wonderful things we have to look forward to in heaven. We are so happy that eternity will be free of death, mourning, tears and pain! We look forward to our life in the new Jerusalem with you and all our brethren. We are no longer afraid, but embrace your sovereign will for us, in Jesus Name, amen.

25
ONE WAY

"I am the way, and the truth, and the life. No one comes to the Father but by me."
John 14:6

A friend knows the song of our hearts and hums it to us when we forget the tune. Lest we forget for an instant the most important principle we must believe if we would properly prepare for a Christian death, let us meditate on this promise given by Jesus to His disciples.

Jesus says "I am the way", "No one comes to the Father except through me." Thomas a Kempis wisely wrote, "without a way no man may go." (Imitation of Christ, 3:55). We do not and cannot reach heaven on our own, without Jesus Christ our head. Jesus is the way in which we ought to go to heaven, through Him and Him alone, for there is no other salvation from sin, death, and hell.

Jesus said "I am the way *and the truth*", "No one comes to the Father except through me." Thomas wrote "without the truth no man may know." Jesus is "the truth which we ought to believe." He is the Son of God, the perfect sacrificial victim, who died to take away the sins of the world. He is the one whose Word is fully trustworthy, and can never fail.

Jesus said "I am the way and the truth *and the life"*, no one comes to the Father except through me." Thomas wrote that "without life no man may live." He is 'the life for which we ought to hope'.

Again Thomas wrote that Jesus is 'the Way that cannot be defiled, the truth which cannot be deceived, and the Life that never shall come to an end."

"No one comes to the Father except through me." These are the Words of the Lord. Let us cleave to them with all our hearts, because "if you confess with your mouth that Jesus is Lord, and believe in your heart that God raised him from the dead, you will be saved"(Rom.10:9).

Holy and precious Lord, we acknowledge that you alone are the one who can save us and bring us through death to eternal life. Help us trust you and believe that you are all who you say you are. We trust you to save us from our sin and take us home to heaven, in your Name, amen.

26

PREPARING FOR DEPARTURE

*"For I am already being poured out as a drink offering, and the time of my
departure has come. I have fought the good fight, I have finished the race, I
have kept the faith. Henceforth there is laid up for me the crown of righteousness, which the Lord, the righteous judge, will award to me on that Day,
and not only to me but also to all who have loved his appearing."*
2 Tim. 4:6-8

Not everyone has the experience of the apostle Paul in this
life. Some of us experience death suddenly without warning,
others may move from this life in a gradual manner, and
others still without any conscious awareness. However, if it is
our privilege to have some time to prepare for death, it does
not come as a surprise, and we might even have a sense of
readiness and excitement at the prospect.

Paul said three things which would give us a great feeling
of closure if we would experience them as well. First, he
said that he had "finished the race." He felt that he had
accomplished all the tasks of ministry that God had called
him to perform. This is a great goal for us.

Secondly, Paul said that he had "kept the faith." He had
been true to the principles and beliefs that Jesus had given
to him, to preach, defend, believe, and even die for. Paul had
been through many earthly trials, but had never faltered in
his faith in Jesus as his Lord. This too, is a wonderful goal for
us as we prepare to go home to be with the Lord.

Third, Paul said that he looked forward to receiving "the crown of righteousness" from the Lord. Paul wanted to go to heaven to receive his reward from the Lord. If this is our goal as well, we can be fruitful every day until we too have an assurance that our day of departure is at hand.

Dear Lord, we thank you for the faith of those who have gone before us. Help us, like Paul, to finish our race, and keep the faith. May we look beyond this life, to see the reward of the life to come, we pray in Jesus Name, amen.

27
GOD WITH US

"Fear not, for I have redeemed you; I have called you by name, you are mine. When you pass through the waters, I will be with you, and through the rivers, they shall not overwhelm you; when you walk through fire you shall not be burned, and the flame shall not consume you. For I am the Lord your God, the Holy one of Israel, your Savior."
Isaiah 43:1b-2

As we reach the final stage of life on this earth, it is important to let God speak to us through His Word. This statement, made by our Lord to his people Israel, is as true today as it was when He uttered it thousands of years ago. In it He reminds us of several important truths, which can comfort us as we cross over to our heavenly homeland.

First, the Lord reminds us that he is our redeemer. He says 'Fear not, for I have redeemed you.' To redeem is to purchase from slavery, to pay a debt. God is the one who has purchased us from the slavery of sin and death. We need fear no condemnation for our sins.

Secondly, the Lord reminds us that we are His possession. He says "I have called you by name, you are mine." We belong to our Lord. He loves us and cherishes us as His own. We can be thankful that we are going home to our heavenly Father.

Thirdly, the Lord promises to be with us throughout our trials of faith. He says: "When you pass through the waters *I will be with you*" (emphasis added). The Lord wants us to know that He will never leave us alone in our trials, but even in the shadow of death, we are to fear no evil, for He is with us (read Psalm 23). Nothing can separate us from God or His love for us (Romans 8). We can never flee to a place that He is not there for us (read Psalm 139). The Lord will be with us during our battle with terminal illness, and will see us through every difficulty.

Fourthly, God will not allow us to be destroyed. He says "when you walk through fire you shall not be burned, and the flame shall not consume you." To those who believe in the Lord, there is no fear of hell, because God loves us.

Fifthly, God is our Savior. He says: "For I am the Lord your God, the Holy One of Israel, your Savior." If we make no attempt to save ourselves, but trust in God as our God and only Savior, we have nothing to fear in death. He is the Sovereign King of the Universe, and no one is able to take us out of His hand (John 10:21).

We can face the horror of death when we know who is with us, who we belong to, and who to depend upon to get us through. Trust in the Lord, dear friend, and you shall pass through the door of death by the grace and goodness of Almighty God, who loves you.

Dear Lord we thank you for being our God and Savior. Thank you for the precious promise that you will be with us as we cross over the water before us. Thank you for taking away from us the fear of death. We love you and praise your Holy Name, amen.

28
GAINING CHRIST

"Indeed, I count everything as loss because of the surpassing worth of knowing Jesus Christ my Lord. For his sake I have suffered the loss of all things and count them as rubbish, in order that I may gain Christ, and be found in him, not having a righteousness of my own that comes from the law, but that which comes through faith in Christ, the righteousness from God that depends on faith."
Phil. 3:8-9

This word of confession is Paul's incredible statement of faith in Jesus Christ. In it he makes clear two great truths, which we can confess as well. First, Paul considered his relationship with Jesus as more important than anything else in the world. He writes: "I count everything as loss because of the surpassing worth of knowing Christ Jesus my Lord." Every part of his life was affected by his confession of Jesus. His family, reputation, racial pedigree, and standing as a Pharisee were all given up for Jesus. He loved the Lord enough to give up his earthly status to serve Him. This is how important Jesus was to Paul, and should be to us.

Secondly, Paul gave up all religious righteousness and observance in favor of accepting by faith the imputed righteousness of Jesus Christ. He, in essence, gave up all works righteousness in favor of trusting in the righteousness which comes by faith in Jesus Christ, our righteous Lord. He did not in any way trust in his own efforts for salvation, but trusted in what Jesus did on the cross as a sacrifice for his sin.

This radical change of life made Paul into a person who honored Christ, not himself. This, too, is something which we can do, as we reject any work of our own as a means of salvation in favor of receiving by faith the finished work of our Lord on the cross as our only means of atonement from sin. Let us emulate this confession of Paul and make it our own, that Jesus may be honored by our faith in Him.

Dear Lord, we acknowledge that we owe our salvation to no pedigree or personal efforts but to your Son our Savior alone. Help us depend on you, and make serving you the goal of the remainder of our lives, we pray in Jesus Name, amen.

29
THE SECRET

"Not that I am speaking of being in need, for I have learned in what-
ever situation I am to be content. I know how to be brought low, and
I know how to abound. In any and every circumstance, I have learned
the secret of facing plenty and hunger, abundance and need. I can do all
things through him who strengthens me."
Phil. 4:11-13

As we wait upon the Lord for our death it is important for us to remain calm and contented, and not grow impatient with the waiting period. Once we have accepted what is to come, we are anxious to see God's promise fulfilled in our lives. How did Paul remain content in the midst of the trials in his life? In this word we are told that his Christian life had been a learning experience, in which he learned how to cope with joys and disappointments, successes and failures. He says: "I have learned the secret of facing plenty and hunger, abundance and need." This is a secret for victory over the ups and downs of our life. It is also a simple truth, which is harder to implement than to understand.

Paul says: "I can do all things through him who strengthens me." Paul dealt with every kind of issue we suffer with. He depended for victory on his relationship with Jesus, who lived in him by His Spirit. Jesus enabled Paul to live a victorious life, because He lived within him and strengthened his inner nature.

Paul never gave any credit to himself for any victory over trials. Rather, he said "we have this treasure in jars of clay, to show that the surpassing power belongs to God and not to us. We are afflicted in every way, but not crushed; perplexed, but not driven to despair; persecuted, but not forsaken; struck down, but not destroyed; always carrying in the body the death of Jesus, so that the life of Jesus may also be manifested in our bodies. For we who live are always being given over to death for Jesus sake, so that the life of Jesus also may be manifested in our mortal flesh" (2 Cor. 4:7-11).

Paul depended on the Lord within him to give him strength for every situation. He gave credit to the Lord alone for his victory over his sufferings.

We too, can trust in Jesus for strength during the ups and downs of our last days on earth. We too, have a treasure in our house of clay. We too, are given over to death, but that death will be only a door to eternal life. May we depend on Jesus for strength in the days ahead, that we might have a sweet, holy death.

Dear Lord, we confess that our struggle and suffering is hard to bear. Thank you for the example of Paul, and his secret of facing his difficult days. Have your way in us, Lord that we might yield to your strength in us, and overcome this trial of our faith, in Jesus Name, amen.

30

COMMITMENT

"Father, into your hands I commit my spirit!"
Luke 23:46

Dear friend, it is my prayer that these meditations on preparing to die have been helpful to you as you have dealt with your final illness. It is my prayer that God's Word would encourage you and feed your faith for the trial you face. God alone knows when He is going to take you home. May He grant you patience and strength as you wait on Him. May he take your pain from you, and grant you rest and peace. May He enable you to see your family and bless them before you go. May He take away all your fears, and grant you courage enough to carry you through this unknown territory. Abide in Jesus, dear friend, for without Him we can do nothing. (John 15:5)

When the time comes, these words Jesus spoke on the cross are as good as any to speak to the Lord as you pass on. He said, 'Father, into your hands I commit my spirit.' Place yourself entirely in His hands, and He will take you home to heaven in peace and joy. Rest in His love for you. Let go of this earth, and open your arms to a hug from heaven. You have loved ones there, you know, who are waiting for you to come, and will be there to greet you, with all the saints who have gone before. But most important, you are going home to be with Jesus in Paradise. He will be there with arms outstretched to take you to his heart. You will see Him, dear one, and you will forget your sorrow and your suffering. You will see him, and all the questions you have ever asked will be answered by the one who will help you understand fully, as you stand face to face with Him. (see I Cor. 13:12) Commit your spirit into the hands of the one who created you. It is only fitting that you go home. Your Father is waiting for you.

Dear Lord, I pray that you will use this your holy Word to comfort and prepare my precious reader for death, that they may enter your kingdom without fear and with great joy. Please bless them and keep them, until we meet one day together, at your throne of grace, I pray in Jesus Name, amen.